THE TEN BIG ANTI-ISRAEL LIES

AND HOW TO REFUTE THEM WITH TRUTH

ALAN DERSHOWITZ

Skyhorse Publishing

Alan Dershowitz Books Relating to Israel, Terrorism, and the Laws of War

War Against the Jews
Defending Israel: The Story of My Relationship with My Most Challenging Client
*The Case Against BDS: Why Singling Out Israel for Boycott Is Anti-Semitic and
    Anti-Peace*
The Case Against the Iran Deal
The Case for Moral Clarity: Israel, Hamas and Gaza
*The Case Against Israel's Enemies: Exposing Jimmy Carter and Others Who Stand
    in the Way of Peace*
Pre-emption: A Knife That Cuts Both Ways
The Case for Peace: How the Arab-Israeli Conflict Can Be Resolved
The Case for Israel
Why Terrorism Works: Understanding the Threat, Responding to the Challenge
Chutzpah

Copyright © 2024 by Alan Dershowitz

All Rights Reserved. No part of this book may be reproduced in any manner
without the express written consent of the publisher, except in the case of brief
excerpts in critical reviews or articles. All inquiries should be addressed to
Skyhorse Publishing, 307 West 36th Street, 11th Floor, New York, NY 10018.

Skyhorse Publishing books may be purchased in bulk at special discounts for
sales promotion, corporate gifts, fund-raising, or educational purposes. Special
editions can also be created to specifications. For details, contact the Special
Sales Department, Skyhorse Publishing, 307 West 36th Street, 11th Floor,
New York, NY 10018 or info@skyhorsepublishing.com.

Skyhorse® and Skyhorse Publishing® are registered trademarks of
Skyhorse Publishing, Inc.®, a Delaware corporation.

Visit our website at www.skyhorsepublishing.com.
Please follow our publisher Tony Lyons on Instagram
@tonylyonsisuncertain.

10 9 8 7 6 5 4 3 2

Library of Congress Cataloging-in-Publication Data is available on file.

Paperback ISBN: 978-1-5107-8354-6
eBook ISBN: 978-1-5107-8355-3

Cover design by Brian Peterson

Printed in the United States of America

Contents

Introduction
An Overview

Vigorous debate about the Israeli-Palestinian conflict, and most recently about the current war against Hamas in Gaza, Hezbollah in Lebanon, and Iran is essential on university campuses and other venues. But what is largely taking place today is not reasoned dialogue. It is shouting, sloganeering, propagandizing, protesting, demonstrating, defunding, accusing, and ignoring or censoring opposing views. The loudest and most disruptive examples of this genre of expression comes from hard-left, woke, progressive, anti-Israel (and anti-American) extremists. Their tactics include blocking access, shouting down, intimidating, and even assaulting those with opposing views.

This book is not primarily about <u>those</u> tactics, some of which are illegal, some simply immoral, and none justifiable as part of the open marketplace of ideas. Instead, this book is about speech that is <u>constitutionally protected</u> but that employs big lies, and that appeals to the ignorance, bias, and follow-the-crowd mentality of so many students and others who have become "useful idiots" in the crusade—or jihad—against the nation-state of the Jewish people. It is based on the premise that false and hateful speech—with some limited exceptions—is protected by the First Amendment, at least, so long as the right of free expression is not selectively applied to the disadvantage of any group. The constitutionally acceptable response to hateful falsehoods is truth and the open marketplace of ideas.

The goal of this book is to contribute to that marketplace by offering truthful and well-documented facts that disprove the defamatory fictions—the big lies—that are pervasive in the current protests against Israel.[1] The book's intended audiences are open-minded students and others who seek to hear fact-based information on all sides of the relevant issues. It is also designed to provide intellectual ammunition to pro-Israel students who seek to engage in exchanges with their anti-Israel interlocutors.

It is hoped that this book will help promote fact-based debate and dialogue about Israel and its enemies. As a lifelong Zionist and supporter—though often a critical supporter—of Israel, I am convinced that the unvarnished truth about all sides of the conflict will, if fairly assessed,

---

1   Those who wish to learn more are encouraged to read my books, in particular, *The Case for Israel* (2003), *The Case for Peace* (2005), *The Case Against the Iran Deal* (2015), and *War Against the Jews* (2023) from which some of the historic material of this short book is adapted and documented with sources.

refute the blood libels currently directed at the nation-state of the Jewish people.

This book will demonstrate that the vast majority of accusations leveled by the anti-Israel protesters and professors are false. In the pages to come, I will describe their ten central accusations about the past, the present, and the future, and then refute them with indisputable documentary, historical, and empirical evidence.

To summarize: The protests against Israel following the massacre of October 7, 2023, are based on falsehoods, bigotry, ignorance, and hatred toward Israel and often America. They are not based on facts. Moreover, they began immediately following the massacre, and before Israel even responded. These rabid protests justified what Hamas had done and blamed Israel. The events <u>following</u> the massacres and rapes of October 7 revealed the depth, breadth, and unthinking ferocity of anti-Israel and anti-Jewish bigotry among so many—especially, but not exclusively, on the hard left.

The pages to come will provide broader contexts for evaluating and refuting the alleged factual underpinnings of the protests. As previously stated, legitimate criticism of some Israeli policies—as well as the policies of all nations—should be encouraged, as it is encouraged in Israel itself. But a fair marketplace of ideas requires that falsehoods be corrected with facts. That is the object of this short book.

Before turning to the specific accusation, it is important to present the big picture of the conflict, and then to address the immediate causes of the current wars in Gaza and Lebanon.

The Big Picture

The indisputable reality is that Israel has always wanted to live in peace on a tiny area of land with few natural resources and borders that are difficult to defend. It has always been a vibrant democracy with a Jewish majority and with equal rights for its Muslim, Christian, and other minorities.

Israel has acquired additional land only as a response to aggressive wars waged against it in 1948, 1967, and 1973. Recently it has sent its troops into the Gaza strip and Lebanon only in response to terrorist attacks, rockets, and other belligerencies.

The Palestinians could have had a state when Israel was established as part of the two-state solution that the United Nations proposed and that the Jews accepted, and the Arabs rejected. In 2000–2001 and 2007, it was offered statehood on 100 percent of the Gaza Strip and 96 percent of the West Bank, with land swaps for 4 percent of current Israel, and with a capital in East Jerusalem.

If Israel's enemies were to stop attacking the nation-state of the Jewish people there would be peace and the prospect of a viable two-state solution, with security for both nations. But the extremist Muslim enemies of Israel are fighting what they believe is a religious war whose goal is the end of Israel as the nation-state of the Jewish people. They believe that their religion forbids them from accepting a non-Muslim political entity in what they regard as Muslim holy land.

The vast majority of Israelis would love nothing more than to be able to beat their swords into plowshares and to convert their nuclear weapons into nuclear medicine. But Israel's enemies do not want peace. They want "Palestine to be free from the river to the sea," which means free of Jews, free of Israel, and free of non-Muslims. They are prepared to use "any means" to secure the result. This would require Israel to commit politicide, which its citizens will not permit it to do.

Unless the world understands this big picture, and why Israel must resist the goals of Hamas, Hezbollah, Iran, and the protesters who support these undemocratic, anti-feminist, Jew-hating, theocratic, terrorist regimes, there can be no real peace. A lasting peace can only be based on the compromises proposed by Israel in 2000–2001 and 2007, which were not accepted by the Palestinian leadership.

Instead of turning against Israel as it has done, the international community and students should turn in favor of a lasting peace that recognizes Israel's right to exist in security as the legitimate nation-state of the Jewish people. Israel can accept no less. And neither should the world. That is the only just road to a realistic solution to this age-old conflict.

The Immediate Causes of the Current Wars

The following points are not subject to rational dispute: 1) had Hamas not broken the cease-fire that was in existence on October 6, 2023, invaded Israel, and murdered 1,200, and kidnapped 250 innocent children, women, and men, there would be no war in Gaza; 2) if Hamas did not employ innocent Gazans as human shields, the death toll among civilians would be considerably lower; 3) if Hamas were to end its belligerence and turn over those responsible for October 7, the war would end; 4) if Hezbollah had not begun to fire thousands of rockets into Israel on October 8 and thereafter, there would be no war in Lebanon; 5) if Israel were to stop defending itself, Hamas would repeat October 7, and Hezbollah would keep firing missiles at Israel. Now to the accusations.

Here, in summary and chronological form, are the protesters' ten central accusations about the past, the present, and the future, and why they are false.

The Past

1) Israel is not a "settler-colonial" state. It was established as a national liberation movement for the Jewish people, who have had a continuous presence in what is now Israel for thousands of years. The Zionist movement successfully fought against both Ottoman and British colonialism and established a vibrant democracy in place of tyrannical colonialist rule.

2) Israel has not denied the Palestinian people statehood. Israel accepted the two-state solution proposed by the UN in 1947–1948, but the Palestinian leadership rejected statehood because it opposed the establishment of any nation-state for the Jewish people, regardless of size. Since

1967, Palestinians have refused to accept resolutions that would have resulted in a Palestinian state on more than 90 percent of the West Bank and the entire Gaza Strip.

3) Israel did not cause the Palestinian refugee problem. Had the Arab states not attacked the new state of Israel in 1948, there would have been no "nakba" and no Palestinian refugees. There would have been a two-state solution in which the Jewish state had a Jewish majority and the Arab state had an Arab majority. Palestinian leaders have exacerbated the problem by creating refugee camps, rather than integrating their fellow Arabs, the way Israel integrated a similar number of Jewish refugees from Arab countries. The United Nations has contributed to the refugee problem by establishing a special agency, UNRWA, that is dedicated to maintaining these camps and the status quo of their residents as "refugees."

The Present

4) Israel is not guilty of apartheid. Israel is a multi-ethnic and multi-religious state in which Arab citizens vote, serve in every branch of the government, and have more civil liberties and human rights than Arabs and Muslims have in any country in the Middle East.

5) Israel is not guilty of genocide. To the contrary, the Israel Defense Forces (IDF) have killed fewer civilians in relation to combatants than any nation in history that has fought against terrorists who use civilians as human shields. Israel is not deliberately "starving" the civilians of

Gaza; it has provided tons of food and medical equipment, much of which Hamas has stolen.

6) The IDF does not target civilians. Israel takes great precautions, including warnings to civilians, precisely to minimize civilian deaths, while Hamas does everything in its power to maximize civilian deaths both among Israelis and Palestinians. Hamas takes innocent civilians as hostages and uses them as human shields in violation of the laws of war. Israel targets terrorist leaders and commanders in Gaza, Lebanon, Iran, and other locations in a successful effort to minimize civilian casualties.

7) The Israeli military presence in the West Bank, Gaza, and Lebanon does not violate international law. It is lawful to maintain a military occupation and presence in captured or enemy territory as long as belligerency continues, as it does throughout the West Bank, Gaza Strip, and Lebanon.

8) Israeli civilian settlements in Gaza (which ended in 2005) and in West Bank may be unwise but their legality or illegality is subject to reasonable dispute under international law. These areas are disputed territories and legal experts disagree as to their status, subject to an agreed-upon resolution. Israel has repeatedly offered to end its occupation of the West Bank (with some land swaps) in exchange for peace. The Palestinian leadership has not accepted these offers.

The Future
9) A two-state solution is possible only if Hamas no longer controls Gaza and Hezbollah no longer dominates

Lebanon. Hamas categorically opposes any resolution that recognizes Israel's right to exist, and insists on their right to destroy the "Zionist entity" by military force, including terrorism of the sort it employed on October 7, 2023, which it has promised to repeat. It wants an exclusively Islamic Palestinian state "from the river to the sea." Most protesters also reject a two-state solution that allows Israel to exist, as does Iran and Hezbollah.

10) Peace in the region is possible only if Iran no longer attacks Israel through its surrogates. Iran demands the right to destroy "the little Satan," Israel, by arming and mobilizing Hezbollah, Hamas, the Houthis, and other terrorist organizations that repeatedly attack Israel. Israel has the right and obligation to repel or preempt these attacks.

There are legitimate criticisms that can be leveled at the Israeli government and its armed forces, just as there are legitimate criticisms against other democracies battling terrorism. But criticism must be based on standards that are equally applicable to all democracies. There cannot be multiple standards based on invidious discrimination. Nor can legitimate criticism be based on distortions of the historical record or the present realities.

Those who make these accusations must recognize the indisputable reality that if Israel's enemies—led by Iran—stopped attacking Israel, there would be peace. If Israel stopped defending itself, there would be genocide. Here then are the detailed responses to the false accusations, but first a note to young defenders of Israel:

A Note to Young Defenders of Israel

This is a heartfelt message to young defenders of Israel on university campuses, in work settings, and elsewhere:

You are a fortunate generation, far more fortunate than previous generations who were not in a position to defend Israel and the Jewish community against anti-Semitism, anti-Zionism, and unfair attacks on your heritage. In the 1930s, students and others your age did not have the power or the ability to speak up against Nazism, fascism, communism, and plain old-fashioned anti-Semitism. They were silenced by their fear, by their lack of status as first-class citizens, and by the absence of real opportunities to compete fairly in the marketplace of ideas.

Your generation, on the other hand, has both the power and the opportunity to defeat the enemies of truth. The attacks on Israel and the Jewish people following the massacres of October 7 have been unprecedented in their viciousness, mendacity, and pervasiveness. But now, as contrasted with the past, there is a relatively open market-place of ideas. Yes, it takes courage to participate openly in that marketplace. You will be attacked, canceled, berated, threatened, downgraded, and punished for telling the truth. But if you have the courage to fight back, you will be rewarded by the verdict of history. Truth, justice, and morality are on your side. Your professors, deans, presidents, and bosses will not have the courage to stand up for what many of them actually believe. You must show the way. You must take the lead. You must speak for the cowards who remain silent.

I wrote this book to help you in the battle for truth. But it is you who must take this truth and enter it into the marketplace of ideas. I, and others in my generation, can help. But the responsibility falls largely to you. In that respect, you are the most fortunate of generations. Take advantage of your good fortunes and speak up—loudly, clearly, and without fear.

I have been advocating for Israel since even before I met Golda Meir, Yitzhak Rabin, and other Israeli leaders in the early 1970s. I wrote *The Case for Israel* in 2003 in order to respond to the lies of that era. But my advocacy represents the past, and perhaps the present. Yours represents the future. And that is most important.

So may you go boldly and without fear from strength to strength.

1. The Accusation: "Israel Is a Colonial, Imperialist State"

The Reality: Israel is the opposite of a colonist imperialist state. Calling Israel a colonial-settler state reflects ignorance, bigotry or both.

Colonialism occurs when one country (e.g. Great Britian or France) colonizes another country (e.g. India or Algeria) and sends its own citizens to become settlers in the colonized country. These settlers have no original connection to the colonized country—they are neither indigenous nor the descendants of indigenous to the colonized country. They are simply sent there to plant the flag of the colonizing country and to exploit the resources for the benefit of the colonizers.

Among the most absurd canards currently being promulgated by protesters against Israel—and used to justify Hamas barbarism—is that Israel is a colonial, settler state, comparable to Imperialist Great Britain and France.

The reality is that Israel is an anti-colonialist democracy comprised primarily of refugees and the descendants of indigenous Jews, Muslims, and Christians exercising their right to political self-determination.

Jews lived in what was originally known as Judea (Yehuda) and then as the land of Israel (Eretz Yisrael) since Biblical times. Unlike the other groups that were indigenous to the land, the Jewish people survived military defeats, exile, and dispersion. Beginning in the 1880s, many Jews who moved to what is now Israel were refugees escaping the oppressive anti-Semitism of colonial Europe and the Muslim states of the Middle East and North Africa. Unlike the colonial settlers serving the expansionist commercial and military goals of imperial nations such as Great Britain, France, the Netherlands, and Spain, the Jewish refugees were escaping from the countries that had oppressed them for centuries. These Jewish refugees were far more comparable to the American colonists who had left England because of religious oppression (or the Europeans who later immigrated to America) than they were to eighteenth- and nineteenth-century English imperialists who colonized India, the French settlers who colonized North Africa, and the Dutch expansionists who colonized Indonesia and Africa.

Those who absurdly claim that the Jewish refugees who immigrated to Palestine in the last decades of the nineteenth century were the "tools" of European imperialism must answer the following question: For whom were these socialists and idealists working? Were they planting the flag of the hated czar of Russia or the anti-Semitic regimes of Poland or Lithuania? These refugees wanted nothing to do with the countries from which they fled to avoid pogroms and religious discrimination. They came to what the Romans had named Palestine, deliberately in order to hide its Jewish origin. They arrived without any of the weapons of imperialism. They brought with them few guns or other means of conquest. Their tools were rakes and hoes. The land they cultivated was not taken away from its rightful owners by force or confiscation by colonial law. It was purchased, primarily from absentee landlords and real estate speculators, at fair or often exorbitant prices.

As Martin Buber, a strong supporter of Palestinian rights, observed in 1939: "Our settlers do not come here as do the colonists from the Occident, to have natives do their work for them; they themselves set their shoulders to the plow and they spend their strength and their blood to make the land fruitful."[1] Nor was the land they sought to cultivate rich in natural resources such as oil or gold, or strategically positioned as a trade route. It was a materially worthless piece of real estate in a backwater of the world whose significance to Jews was religious, historical, and familial.

Moreover, as the British historian Paul Johnson has documented, the colonial powers did everything possible to thwart the establishment of a Jewish homeland:

---

1   Buber to Gandhi, quoted in Arthur Herzberg, *The Zionist Idea* (Philadelphia, Jewish Publication Society, 1997), p. 464.

"Everywhere in the West, the foreign offices, defense ministries, and big business were against the Zionists."[2] The Jewish refugees who came to live in Palestine had to overcome Turkish, British, and Pan-Arab imperialism and colonialism in order to achieve self-determination.

The Jewish refugees from Europe joined the mostly Sephardic Jews who had lived in Palestine for generations. The first wave of European immigration (or Aliyah, as it was called), beginning in 1882 and ending in 1903, was not very different in many respects from the first large-scale immigration of Eastern European Jews to America at about the same time. This was an era of massive emigration and immigration throughout the world, especially from the crowded cities and towns of Europe. Enormous population shifts took place, with people settling in places far away from their birthplaces. Irish, Italian, Greek, German, Polish, and Jewish families as well as Chinese, Japanese, and Caribbean families, sought better lives in the United States, Canada, South America, Australia, and other places where they could work with their hands and develop their minds.

Approximately ten thousand Eastern European Jews immigrated to Palestine during that period as compared to nearly a million Jews who immigrated to the United States. The Jews of the First Aliyah produced a manifesto in 1882, in which they explicitly referred to the recent

---

2   Paul Johnson, *Modern Times: The World from the Twenties to the Nineties* (New York: Harper & Row, 1983), p. 485.

wave of pogroms as well as the more distant *autos-da-fé* that had threatened to destroy European Jewry. Like the Jews who sought refuge in America, most of the Jews who first returned to Zion were simply looking for a place to live in peace, without discrimination and without physical threats to their survival. They certainly had that right.

Palestine, or as it has been known to Jews for centuries, Eretz Yisrael, was the land of their forebears. It was an appropriate refuge destination for several important reasons, including that there has always been a significant Jewish presence in Palestine. These refugees, who joined their fellow Jews who were among the indigenous population, were not there on behalf of any other nation. They were there on behalf of the National Liberation Movement of the Jewish People.

Palestine, with its relatively small population, was never without a significant and well-documented Jewish presence. By the time the Ottoman Turks occupied Palestine in 1516, approximately ten thousand Jews lived in the Safed region alone. In the sixteenth century, according to British reports, "as many as 15,000 Jews" lived in Safed which was "a center of rabbinical learning."[3] Many more Jews lived in Jerusalem, Hebron, Acre, and other locations. Jerusalem, in fact, has had a Jewish majority since the first population figures were gathered in the early nineteenth century. According to the British consul in

---

3 *Palestine Royal Commission Report* (*Peel Report*) (London: His Majesty's Stationary Office, 1937), pp. 11-12.

Jerusalem, the Muslims of Jerusalem "scarcely exceed[ed] one quarter of the whole population."[4]

Jerusalem was a predominantly Jewish city well before the First Aliyah by European Jews. By the middle of the nineteenth century—thirty years before the First Aliyah—Jews also constituted a significant presence, often a plurality or majority, in Safed, Tiberias, and several other cities and towns. Tel Aviv has been a predominantly Jewish city since European Jews founded it on sand dunes in 1909.

At about the time the first wave of European Jewish refugees were immigrating to Palestine, other waves of Jewish refugees from Muslim countries such as Yemen, Iraq, Turkey, and North Africa were also beginning to arrive in Palestine. These Arab Jews had little knowledge of political Zionism. They were simply returning home to escape persecution, having learned that the Ottoman Empire was permitting (or closing its eyes to) some Jewish immigration into Palestine. At the same time, many Arabs from what is now Syria, Lebanon, Jordan, and Egypt moved to Palestine—some to work in Jewish wineries and other businesses.

Based on the actual history of the Jewish refugees who immigrated to Palestine, the claim that Israel is a colonial or imperialist state is so farfetched that it simply serves to illustrate how language is willfully distorted in the service of a partisan agenda.

Contrast the millennia-long Jewish presence in

---

4   James Finn to Earl of Clarendon, January 1, 1958.

Palestine to the lack of presence or history of English settlers sent to places like New Zealand by Great Britain as
part of its colonial enterprise. New Zealand is a perfect
example of a colonialist-settler state. Israel is the opposite.
Calling Israel a colonial-settler state is a reflection of ignorance, bigotry, or both.

2. The Accusation: "Israel Denied Statehood to the Palestinian People"

The Reality: Israel offered Palestinian statehood in 1937–1938, 1947–1948, 1967, 1993, 2000–2001, and 2007 and each time the Palestinian leadership refused.

It is a lie to claim that Israel has denied statehood to the Palestinian people. To the contrary, Israel agreed to Palestinian statehood in 1937–1938, 1947–1948, 1967, 1993, 2000–2001, and 2007. In each case, it was the Palestinian leadership that refused to agree to the two-state solution that would have created a Palestinian state, alongside a state for its Jewish inhabitants.

In 1937—in the midst of the terrorist revolt inspired by the Grand Mufti of Jerusalem—the British published the *Palestine Royal Commission Report* (also known as the *Peel Commission Report* or the *Peel Report*), based on its investigation of the "causes of the disturbances." It left no doubt about who was at fault: "one side put itself, not for the first time, in the wrong by resorting to force, whereas the other side patiently kept the law."[5] The Commission realized that the murderous violence against civilians that had begun in the 1920s had been deliberately ordered by the mufti and the Arab high committee. It also confirmed that the Jews who had come to Palestine were refugees, calling Zionism "a creed of escape" from the persecution suffered by the Jews of the Diaspora. In the broadest sense, it saw the problem as "fundamentally a conflict of right with right" that was rooted deeply in the past. After reviewing the historic claims of the Jews and the Arabs, the Commission found them both compelling.

The Peel Commission found that "the sympathy of the Palestinian Arabs within their kinsmen in Syria had been plainly shown. . . . Both people clung to the principle that Palestine was part of Syria and should never have been cut off from it." It also found that it would be "wholly unreasonable to expect" the Jews to accept minority status in a Muslim state, especially since they had essentially created a Jewish Home, with Hebrew newspapers, Hebrew schools and universities, a Jewish hospital system, an active political and labor union system, and all the other attributes of statehood. The Jewish areas of Palestine were more like an ongoing state than were the Arab areas. Tel Aviv was a Jewish metropolis with a population exceeding 150,000. West Jerusalem had a Jewish population of

---

5   *Palestine Royal Commission Report* (*Peel Report*) (London, His Majesty's Stationary Office, 1937), p. 2.

seventy-six thousand, far exceeding the Muslim population. Haifa, with its population of one hundred thousand, was half Jewish, and much of the business at its port "is Jewish business." Local democratic governments, as well as a national agency, featured nearly twenty political parties. Democracy had come to the Jewish areas of Palestine. So had Jewish art and culture.

In 1937, the Peel Commission recommended a partition plan by which to resolve what it characterized as an "irrepressible conflict . . . between two national communities within the narrow bounds of one small country." Because of the general hostility and hatred of the Jews by the Muslims, "national assimilation between Arabs and Jews is . . . ruled out." Nor could the Jews be expected to accept Muslim rule over them, especially since the grand mufti made it clear that most of the Jews would be transferred out of Palestine if the Muslims gained complete control. The Peel Commission concluded that partition was the only solution.[6]

---

6   Manifestly, the problem cannot be solved by giving either the Arabs or the Jews what they want. The answer to the question "Which of them in the end will govern Palestine?" must surely be "Neither." We do not think that any fair-minded statesman would suppose, now that the hope of harmony between the races has provided untenable, that Britain ought either to hand over to Arab rule four hundred thousand Jews...or that if the Jews should become a majority, a million or so of Arabs should be handed over to their rule. But, while neither race can justly rule all Palestine, we see no reason why, if it were practicable, each race should not rule part of it. Partition seems to offer at least a chance of ultimate peace. We can see none in any other plan.

The Peel Commission plan proposed a Jewish home in areas in which there was a clear Jewish majority. Divided into two noncontiguous sections, the northern portion extended from Tel Aviv to the current border with Lebanon. It consisted largely of a ten-mile-wide strip of land from the Mediterranean east to the end of the coastal plain, then a somewhat wide area from Haifa to the Sea of Galilee. A southern portion, disconnected from the northern one by a British-controlled area that includes Jerusalem, with its majority Jewish population, extended from south Jaffa to north of Gaza.

The proposed Arab area was, on the other hand, entirely contiguous and encompassed the entire Negev, the West Bank, and the Gaza Strip. It was many times larger than the proposed Jewish home. The population of the proposed Jewish area would have included 300,000 Jews and 190,000 Arabs. More than 75,000 additional Jews lived in Jerusalem, which would have remained under British control.

The commission also alluded to how partition would help the rescue of Europe's Jews from Nazism.

The Jews reluctantly accepted the Peel partition plan, while the Arabs categorically rejected it, demanding that all of Palestine be placed under Arab control and that most of the Jewish population of Palestine be "transferred" out of the country, because "this country [cannot] assimilate the Jews now in the country."[7] The Peel Commission

---

7   *Peel Report*, p. 114.

implicitly recognized that it was not so much that the Arabs wanted self-determination as that they did not want the Jews to have self-determination or sovereignty over the land the Jews themselves had cultivated and in which they were a majority. The Palestinians wanted to be part of Syria and be ruled over by a distant monarch. They simply could not abide the reality that the Jews of Palestine had created for themselves a democratic homeland pursuant to the League of Nations mandate and binding international law. Even if turning down the Peel proposal resulted in no state for the Palestinians, that was preferable to allowing even a tiny, noncontiguous state for the Jews. When the British convened a meeting between the parties, "the Arabs would not sit in the same room as the Jews." Further, they responded to the Peel plan with massive violence directed at Jewish civilians, as well as at British police and civil servants.[8]

---

8   This impasse, resulting from Arab rejection of "all attempts to give any part of Palestine over to Jewish sovereignty," coupled with Arab violence, led directly to the British decision to curtail the flow of Jewish refugees into Palestine, despite acknowledgement in the *Peel Commission Report* that "Jews enter Palestine as of right and not on sufferance," and that Jewish Immigration is "not merely sanctioned but required by solemn international agreements." The British White Paper of 1939 limited Jewish immigration to seventy-five thousand over the next five years. Britian had become the barrier to independence and statehood for the Jewish community in Palestine. British imperialistic goals now favored the Arabs over the Jews. It was the Arab, not the Jewish population of Palestine, that were the beneficiaries of colonialism.

Following the end of World War II, the United Nations also recommended partition of the area into two states—one for the Arab population, the other for the Jewish population. Once again, the Arab leadership rejected the two-state solution, while the Jewish leadership accepted it. The Jewish leadership declared statehood in the area allocated to it by the UN. The Arab leadership responded by declaring a genocidal war against the new state of the Jewish people. They did not want a Palestinian state. And they wanted there to be no Jewish state.

As soon as Israel declared its independence, Egypt, Jordan, Syria, Iraq, and Lebanon attacked it, with help from Saudi Arabia, Yemen, and Libya. Arab armies, with the help of Palestinian terrorists, determined to destroy the new Jewish state and exterminate its population.

The first attack on Israel came from the air. Egyptian aircraft bombed Israel's largest civilian center, the city of Tel Aviv. An Associated Press account on May 17, 1948, described the attack: "Arab Planes Hit Tel Aviv, Tiberias; Invader Hammering Jewish Outposts."[9] As with virtually every previous Arab attack against the Jews since the first refugees arrived in Palestine—and even before—the targets were innocent civilians.

The pattern of past and future fighting was thus established: the Arabs would target soft civilian areas—cities, towns, kibbutzim, and moshavim—trying to kill as many

---

9   Associated Press report published in *The Morning Call*, Allentown, Pa., May 17, 1948.

children, women, elderly, and other unarmed civilians as possible, while the Israelis would respond by targeting soldiers, military equipment, and other lawful targets.

The Egyptians and Jordanians also captured land, for no reason other than to increase their own territory and to control their Palestinian residents. Indeed, by the end of the war, according to historian Benny Morris, the "Arab war Plan changed . . . into a multinational land grab focusing on the Arab areas of the country. The evolving Arab 'plans' failed to assign any of these whatsoever to the Palestinians or to consider their political aspirations."[10]

A key part of the Arab plan was the complete "marginalization" of the Palestinians. The Jordanians wanted the West Bank, and the Egyptians wanted the Gaza Strip. Neither wanted an independent Palestinian state. Nobody can blame Israel for the Egyptian and Jordanian decision to occupy the lands allocated to the Palestinians for a state and for denying the Palestinians the right of self-determination in those lands. These are incontrovertible historical facts not subject to reasonable dispute but omitted from pro-Palestinian pseudo-histories of the period. The occupation of Palestine by Jordan and Egypt was never the subject of UN condemnation or even expression of concern from human rights groups. Indeed, it was not even widely protested by Palestinians.

After the Six-Day-War of 1967, which resulted in Israel

---

10 Benny Morris, *Righteous Victims* (New York: Vintage Books), p. 221.

capturing the West Bank, Gaza Strip, and East Jerusalem, Israel signaled its willingness to negotiate land for peace. However, the Arab League met in Khartoum and issued the infamous "Three No's": no peace with Israel, no recognition of Israel, and no negotiations with Israel. This led Israel's ambassador to the United Nations, Abba Eban, to quip: "I think that this is the first war in history that has ended with the victors suing for peace and the vanquished calling for unconditional surrender."[11]

According to former President Bill Clinton, the Israelis, in 2000–2001, offered to withdraw from approximately 96 percent of the West Bank and 100 percent of the Gaza Strip in exchange for peace. The Palestinians were offered land swaps from Israel in exchange for the small amount of land that would remain under Israeli control. Yasser Arafat rejected that offer and initiated a series of terrorist attacks that left thousands dead. In 2007, Prime Minister Ehud Olmert offered an even better deal. Once again, the Palestinian leadership did not accept the offer. As one Israeli leader put it, "The Palestinians don't know how to take yes for an answer."

It is therefore incorrect to claim that Israel denied the Palestinians statehood. The Palestinian leadership did.

The Palestinians deserve to have a state, but their claim is no greater than that of the Tibetans, the Kurds, the Chechens, and other stateless groups. Indeed, these other groups, unlike the Palestinians, have never been

---

11   Abba Eban, *Abba Eban* (New York: Random House, 1977), p. 446.

offered statehood and turned it down. Nor would these groups refuse to sit down and negotiate for a state.

The two-state solution would be good for the Palestinians, for Israel, and for peace in the region. But it is the Palestinians who need it most. They are demanding of Israel substantial territorial compromises. They are also demanding prisoner releases, an end to construction in the settlements, and a termination of Israel's military presence in the vulnerable Jordan Valley. To get these and other concessions from Israel, the Palestinians and their allies must be prepared to make sacrifices as well. And they must assure Israel's security against attacks from within the areas under their control. The attacks on October 7 in Gaza, October 8 and thereafter from Lebanon, and more recent attacks in April and October 2024 from Iran, show that they are either unable or unwilling to do so.

3. The Accusation: "Israel Caused the Refugee Problem of the Palestinians"

The Reality: Israel did not cause the refugee problem. The Arab leadership created it, maintained it, and exploited it for political gain.

Israel did not cause the refugee problem. The Arab leadership created it, exploited it, and maintained it to this day. Had the Arab armies not attacked the newly established state of Israel, there would have been no Palestinian refugees. The Palestinian population of the new state would have remained in their homes and villages. The Palestinian population of Israel at that time was approximately 950,000. Now, even after many left and became refugees,[12] Palestinians form a large segment of the 1.2 million Arabs living in Israel today.

---

12 Most prominent scholars have put the number of Palestinian refugees anywhere from 472,000 to 750,000. See *The Case for Israel*, Ch. 12.

Had the Arab armies won, there would have been genocide because the grand mufti declared "a holy war" and ordered his "Muslim brothers" to "murder the Jews. Murder them all."[13] There were to be no survivors or refugees. The position of the grand mufti had always been that an Arab Palestine could not absorb even four hundred thousand Jews. By 1948 the Jewish population exceeded six hundred thousand. Extermination, not the creation of a difficult refugee population, was the goal of the Arab attack on Jewish civilian populations. As the Arab League secretary general Abd al-Ahlman Azzah Pasha, candidly put it, "this will be a war of extermination and momentous massacre, which will be spoken of like the Mongolian massacres and the Crusades."[14] The grand mufti's spokesman, Ahmad Shukeiry, called for "the elimination of the Jewish state" with regard to the goal of the Arab attack. There was no talk of, or planning for, a large Jewish refugee population in the event of an Arab victory. "It does not matter how many Jews there are. We will sweep them into the sea,"[15] the Arab league secretary general announced. The Jews fully understood that they "faced slaughter should they be defeated."[16]

Israel, on the other hand, was prepared to extend full

---

13 Larry Collins and Dominique Lapierre, *O Jerusalem* (New York: Simon & Schuster, 1972), p. 400.

14 Quoted in Alan Dershowitz, *The Case for Israel*, p. 81 (2003).

15 Morris, p. 219.

16 Morris, p. 223.

citizenship to whatever number of Arabs remained in the Jewish state. Although many Jews surely preferred a smaller, rather than a larger, Arab minority, the official Jewish organizations took no steps to assure a reduction in the Arab population in general, albeit Israeli military commanders did order the evacuation of several hostile towns that had served as bases for Arab irregular units, which were preventing access to the main road to Jerusalem and which "proved the permanent threat to all north-south and to east-west (Tel Aviv-Jerusalem) communications."[17]

---

17 Another phase of the Arab refugee problem took place when the Haganah won the battle for Haifa at the end of April 1948. According to Morris, "the Arab leaders, preferring not to surrender, announced that they and their community intended to evacuate the town, despite a plea by the Jewish mayor that they stay." Similarly, in Jaffa, the fierce fighting with many Jewish casualties caused a panic among the town's Arab population and many fled. David Ben-Gurion wrote in his diary, "I couldn't understand. Why did the inhabitants . . . leave?"

Of course, Jaffa remained an Arab city, and today its population includes thousands of Arabs. Haifa remained a mixed city, whose current population also includes thousands of Arabs. Some other towns and villages from which Arabs fled remain mixed today, while some have not seen a return of Arab populations. Benny Morris, who is harshly critical of traditional Israeli history with regard to the refugee issue, summarizes the problem caused by the Palestinian and Pan-Arab attack: "The Palestinian Refugee problem was born of war, not by design . . . the Arab leadership inside and outside Palestine probably helped precipitate the exodus . . . No guiding hand or central control is evident." Morris states that "[d]uring the first month, the flight of the middle and upper classes from the towns provoked little Arab interest."

In his 1972 memoirs, the former Prime Minister of Syria, Khalid al-Azm, placed the entire blame for the refugee problem on the Arabs:

> Since 1948 it is we who demanded the return of the refugees . . . while it is we who made them leave . . . we brought disaster upon . . . Arab refugees, by inviting them and bringing pressure to bear upon them to leave . . . we have rendered them dispossessed . . . we have accustomed them to begging . . . we have participated in lowering their moral and social level . . . Then we exploited them and executing crimes of murder, arson, and throwing bombs upon . . . men, women and children dash all this in the service of political purposes.[18]

Even Mahmoud Abbas, the Prime Minister of the Palestinian Authority, has accused the Arab armies of having abandoned the Palestinians after they "forced them to emigrate and to leave their homeland and threw them into prisons similar to the ghettos in which the Jews used to live."[19]

Other sources sympathetic to the Arab cause agree. In 1980, the Arab national committee of Haifa wrote a

---

18 Quoted in Bernard Harrison, *Blaming the Jews: Politics and Delusion* (Indiana University Press 2020), p. 188.

19 "Abu Mazen Charges That Arab States Are the Cause of the Palestinian Refugee Problem," *Wall Street Journal*, June 5, 2003.

memorandum to the Arab states that included the following: "The removal of the Arab inhabitants . . . was voluntary and was carried out at our request. The Arab delegation proudly asked for the evacuation of the Arabs and their removal to the neighboring Arab countries . . . we are very glad to state that the Arabs guarded their honor and traditions with pride and greatness." And a research report by the Arab-sponsored Institute for Palestine Studies concluded that the majority of the Arab refugees were not expelled, and 68 percent of them "left without seeing an Israeli soldier."[20] At the very least, the issue is too complex and multifaceted for simple finger-pointing, and only in one direction.

The United Nations, recognizing that many of the refugees had not lived for long in the villages they left, made a remarkable decision to change the definition of refugee— *only* for purposes of defining who is an Arab refugee *from Israel*—to include any Arab who had lived in Israel for *two years* before leaving. Moreover, an Arab was counted as a refugee if he moved just a few miles from one part of Palestine to another—even if he *returned* to the village in which he had previously lived and in which his family still lived, from a village to which he had moved only two years earlier. Indeed, a significant number of Palestinian refugees simply moved from one part of Palestine to another. Some

---

20 Peter Dodd & Halim Barakat, *River Without Bridges: A Study of the Exodus of the 1967 Palestinian Arab Refugees* (Institute for Palestine Studies, 1969), p. 43.

preferred to live in an area controlled by Arabs rather than Jews, just as the Jews who had lived in cities that came under Arab control chose to move to the Israeli side of the partition. The Jews who moved a few miles (even those who had no choice) were not called refugees, but the Arabs who moved the same distance were. It was the most unusual definition of refugee in history.

Unlike all other refugees worldwide, Palestinian refugees are treated to a separate UN agency, with a separate definition of refugee and a separate mission. If the standard definition of refugee (which applies to all other refugee groups) were to apply to the Palestinians, the number of Palestinian refugees would fall precipitously.

This approach to the refugee issue was calculated to keep it from being resolved and to allow it to fester and even be exacerbated. The Arab refugee problem could easily have been solved between 1948 and 1967 when Jordan controlled and annexed the West Bank, which was an underpopulated and under-cultivated area. But instead of integrating the refugees into a religiously, linguistically, and culturally identical society, they were segregated into ghettos called refugee camps and made to live on the UN dole, while being fed propaganda about their glorious return to the village down the road that had been their home for as little as two years.

At about the same time that 472,000 to 750,000 Arabs became refugees from Israel, tens of millions of other refugees had been created as the result of World War II. In virtually all of those cases, the refugees were displaced from locations in which they and their ancestors had lived for decades, sometimes centuries—certainly more than the two years required for being considered a Palestinian refugee. For example, the Sudeten Germans, who were moved *en masse* out of the borderlands of Czechoslovakia, had lived there for hundreds of years. The Jews of Europe—what remained of them after the Holocaust—had lived in Poland, Germany, Czechoslovakia, Hungary, and the Soviet Union for hundreds of years.

As the result of having lived in what became Israel for as little as two years, thousands upon thousands of Arabs and their descendants have been kept in refugee camps for three-quarters of a century to be used as political pawns in an effort to demonize and destroy Israel. During that same period of time, many other refugee problems in the world have been solved by the host nations accepting and integrating the refugee population into their own. Exchanges of population took place between several nations—including India and Pakistan, and Greece and Turkey—without the need to build permanent refugee camps. Although those exchanges were not without difficulties and some remain controversial, none has created the kind of enduring problems caused by the unwillingness of Arab states to integrate the Palestinian Arab population.

Between 1948 and 1967, tens of millions of other refugees became productive members of their new societies. Yet for the nearly twenty years that Egypt and Jordan controlled the Gaza Strip and the West Bank, the Palestinian refugee population remained in camps, growing in size and desperation. Even King Hussein of Jordan, who could have helped solve the refugee problem, acknowledged that the Arab nations have used the Palestinian refugees as pawns since the beginning of the conflict: "Since 1948 Arab leaders . . . have used the Palestine people for selfish political purposes. This is . . . criminal."[21]

The other major refugee problem that affected the Middle East was the creation of hundreds of thousands of Jewish refugees from Arab and Muslim countries in which they had lived for hundreds or sometimes thousands of years, even before the advent of Islam. Mohammed and his contemporaries created a refugee problem when they banned Jews from Arabia. Then again after the creation of the Jewish state, the situation of Jews in many Arab and Muslim countries became so fraught with risk that many felt they had no choice but to leave. In the years following the establishment of the state of Israel, as many as 750,000 so-called Arab Jews became refugees from the lands in which they had been born. The number of Jewish refugees from Arab lands was not very different than the number of Arab refugees from Israel.

There was "an exchange of populations," with the Jewish refugees having been forced to abandon far more of their property and wealth than the refugees left behind. Those abandoned assets included large houses, businesses, and cash. The difference is that Israel worked hard

---

21 "Hussein Critical of Arab Leaders; Jordan King Says Refugees Are Used As 'Pawns,'" *New York Times*, Jan. 18, 1960.

(although not always with complete success) to integrate its refugee population into the mainstream, while the Arabs deliberately encouraged Arab refugees to fester by keeping so many of them in camps, where many still remain, and refusing to integrate them into their more homogeneous populations. This was done purely to try to cast doubt on Israel's legitimacy despite the desperate need in some underpopulated Arab countries, such as Syria and Jordan, for more workers to serve the labor-intensive economic needs of those nations.

Sabri Jiryis, a former Arab-Israeli lawyer who left Israel and became a member of the Palestinian National Council, has acknowledged that "the Jews of the Arab states were driven out of their ancient homes [and] shamefully deported after their property had been commandeered. [W]hat happened was a . . . population and property exchange, and each party must bear the consequences. . . . [T]he Arab states . . . must settle the Palestinians in their own midst and solve their problems. Instead, they deliberately exacerbated the problems."

To understand how different the Arab-Israeli conflict would look if the Arab world, including the Palestinian Muslims, had accepted the two-state solution when it was first proposed (or even for years thereafter), we must briefly return to the *Peel Commission Report*. If the Arabs had accepted the Peel Commission partition proposal, there would have been a Palestinian state (in addition to Transjordan) in most of what was left of Palestine following the partition of Transjordan. The vast majority of

Arabs and Muslims in Palestine would have lived under Palestinian control, and the Arab minority that lived in the land allotted to the Jewish state would have had the choice to move to the Palestinian state or remain as part of the Arab minority in the Jewish state. The same would have been true for the Jews who lived in the Arab state.

The Jewish state would have been open to immigration and could have saved hundreds of thousands, perhaps even more, European Jews from the Holocaust. Although the area allotted to the Jewish state by the Peel Commission was tiny in comparison with that allotted to the Arab state (and comparably even smaller if Transjordan is included), it was large enough to absorb millions of refugees, as evidenced by the fact that millions of people live within that area today.

There would have been no Arab refugee problem had the Arab states accepted the subsequent UN partition. But instead, having rejected Jewish self-determination in 1937, the Arab world rejected it once again in 1948 and attacked Israel in an effort to destroy the new Jewish state, exterminate its Jewish population, and drive the Jews into the sea. Then again in 1967, it threatened Israel with destruction and annihilation, causing yet other refugee and territorial problems. Now, Palestinian leaders and their allies, including the UN and especially UNRWA, seek to maintain the refugee status of millions of Palestinians as a weapon against the legitimacy of Israel.

4. The Accusation: "Israel Is an Apartheid State!"

The Reality: Israel is not an apartheid state. To the contrary, it is the most ethically, religiously, and racially diverse and democratic entity in the Middle East. Arab and Muslim citizens vote, have political parties, hold high office and, with a few exceptions, have equal rights as their Jewish compatriots.

Apartheid is a term derived from the racial policies of South Africa between 1948 and 1990, where a small minority of whites from England and the Netherlands ruled over, and segregated by law, its majority of Blacks, who were forbidden to vote, hold office, or live in certain areas. It was even worse than the post-civil war "Jim Crow" laws in the American South.

Under Israeli law, on the other hand, Arab and Muslim citizens vote, have political parties, hold high office and, with a few exceptions such as mandatory military service and the law of return, have equal rights as a matter of enforceable law. It was an Arab judge who sentenced Israel's former president to prison. It was an Arab prison guard who watched over the former Prime Minister of Israel while he served his sentence. Arab professors teach Jews, Arabs, and Christians in Israeli universities; Arab doctors treat Jewish patients; and Arab voters influence Knesset elections and votes. The Israeli hostage rescued near the end of August was a Muslim Bedouin. Israelis cheered his rescue as joyously as if he had been a Jew.

This is not apartheid. And it diminishes the horror of real apartheid to misuse and trivialize that term to characterize Israel's vibrant and diverse, if imperfect, democracy.

To be sure, there are some differences—both legal and practical—between the status of Jewish and Arab citizens. Jewish citizens are required to serve in the IDF. (The ultra-religious *haredim* were exempt from military service until the Israeli High Court, in the aftermath of the October 7 attacks, changed that in a June 2024 decision.) Arab citizens are not required, but may volunteer, as many Bedouin and Druze citizens do. It is not apartheid to grant Arab and Muslim citizens the right not to be compelled to fight against the Arab and Muslim enemies of Israel. It is a recognition of the reality of the human condition.

The same is true of the law of return, which recognizes the historic reality of the Holocaust and the refusal of virtually all the nations of the world to accept Jewish refugees seeking to escape the Nazi gas chambers. Israel was established in large part as a place of asylum for Jews. Its first law authorized any Jew to seek asylum from, or make aliya to, the nation-state of the Jewish people. Others too could seek asylum in Israel, and many have, but all Jews are welcome as matter of right, based on the tragic history of being refused asylum by the United States, Canada, Great Britain, and most of the rest of the world, before, during, and even after the worst genocide in history.

The law of return, which includes non-Jewish relatives of Jews, was instrumental in rescuing Jews from post-World War II persecution in Arab and Muslim countries, as well as in the Soviet Union. Even now, Jews from European countries, including France, are taking advantage of the law of return to escape increasing anti-Semitism.

If, someday, anti-Semitism ceases to exist throughout the world, there might be occasion to reconsider or amend the current law of return, but this is surely not the time to do so, with Jew-hatred increasing even in countries like the United States, Great Britain, Canada, Australia, and other places.

Although history provides Israel with the most powerful justification for having a law of return, it is not the only nation to have such a law. Other countries—such as Germany, China, and France—grant automatic entry, citizenship, or preference to individuals who have ethnic, nationalistic, religious, familial, historic, or other ties to their population. To single out Israel for criticism—and especially to accuse it of apartheid, because of its historically justified law of return—is to apply an invidious double standard to the nation-state of the Jewish people. (In fact, the most primitive apartheid against non-Muslims is still openly practiced in some Arab countries. Jordan, for instance, has a law of return that explicitly denies citizenship to all Jews, even those who lived there for generations. Saudi Arabia similarly bases eligibility for a right of return on religious affiliation. Yet no one accuses Jordan or Saudia Arabia of apartheid.)

Some critics of Israel concede that Israel proper is not guilty of apartheid, but they accuse Israel of practicing the equivalent of apartheid on the West Bank, where different laws are applicable to Israelis who live in West Bank settlements and Arabs who reside in West Bank cities and villages. For example, a widely circulated canard claims that there are separate roads for Jews and Arabs. That is demonstrably false. It is true, that for security reasons, there are separate roads for Israelis, on the one hand, and for non-Israelis who live on the West Bank. But the roads for Israelis are open to all Arab and other non-Jewish citizens of Israel. This is different from some roads in Saudi Arabia that are restricted to Muslim only.

It is automatic that when a nation occupies areas, the residents of those areas are not citizens of the occupying nation, and do not have the same rights as the citizens of the occupying nation. The difference is inherent in the very nature of an occupation. That is not apartheid; it is occupation. And if and when the occupation ends, the disparate treatment ends as well. When Egypt occupied the Gaza strip and Jordan occupied the West Bank between 1948 and 1967, the residents of those occupied territories did not have all the same rights as the citizens of the occupying nations. Yet no one accused Egypt of apartheid. Israel has repeatedly offered to end its occupations in exchange for peace and mutual recognition, but the Palestinian leadership has refused to accept these offers.

Indeed, in 2005 Israel completely ended its occupation of the Gaza Strip and turned control of that area to the Palestinian Authority, which was then replaced in a bloody coup by Hamas. The result has been fewer rights for the residents of the Gaza Strip than they had under the Israeli occupation.

The truth is that Israel cannot legitimately be accused of apartheid. It is far from perfect in its dealings with its Arab minorities in Israel proper or the West Bank. In this respect, it is far closer to the United States, Great Britain, France, the Netherlands, Sweden, and other Western democracies in how they deal with minorities than it is to how white South Africa dealt with its majority Black population. To accuse Israel of apartheid is to distort the meaning of that term and to demean the history and suffering of South African Blacks who were forced to live—and die—under real apartheid.

5. The Accusation: "Israel Is Guilty of Genocide and War Crimes"

The Reality: Israel is not guilty of genocide, war crimes, or starvation. To the contrary, it has done more to protect the civilians of Gaza and Lebanon than any nation that has fought against terrorists who use their civilians as human shields to protect their combatants.

Critics of Israel have charged the Jewish state with committing atrocities and even "genocide" in its ongoing war with Hamas and Hezbollah. The South African government has brought these charges before the International Court of Justice. The accusations are without merit: Israel has committed no war crimes in seeking to degrade and destroy Hamas in Gaza and Hezbollah in Lebanon. Hamas and Hezbollah, directed by Iran, by contrast, has committed at least four categories of war crimes.

First, Hamas waged an aggressive war against Israel, crossing its border and murdering, raping, and kidnapping civilians. Hezbollah and Iran have fired thousands of rockets at Israel. Second, they have targeted civilians with its rockets. Third, they have dressed terrorists in civilian clothing, thus eliminating the important distinction between combatants and civilians. And fourth, they have used civilians as human shields.

Unlike Hamas and Hezbollah, which began this war, Israel has acted in self-defense. Under international law, it has the right and obligation to defend its citizens by all reasonable and lawful means.

In doing so, the Israel Defense Forces have made extraordinary efforts to target only combatants. Notwithstanding these efforts, Palestinian civilians have been killed, largely because Hamas has deliberately embedded its war machinery among civilians precisely in order to produce dead bodies to display to the media.

Hamas-controlled health authorities have claimed that more than forty thousand Palestinians have been killed thus far. But they have not distinguished between combatants and civilians. Israel claims to have killed approximately seventeen thousand combatants. Hamas claims that many of those killed were children and women. But they have not revealed the ages of the dead "children," whom the terror group defines as anyone under nineteen. Hamas actively recruits terrorists from the age of thirteen. This brutal strategy, itself a war crime, raises discomfiting questions about Hamas's fatality claims: an eighteen-year-old with an RPG or an assault weapon is as much a combatant as a thirty-year-old, even if Hamas categorizes him or her as a "child."

The same is true of women. Hamas regards women as incapable of performing many roles, but one role many are recruited to perform is that of terrorist and combatant. And so it cannot be assumed that all of the women who have been killed were civilians. It is clear that some were combatants who were complicit in terrorism.

Then there are those who have been killed by "friendly fire"—including misfired rockets and bullets fired by Hamas against Palestinians who were trying to flee to safe areas.

Although it is impossible to know for certain how many actually innocent civilians have been killed, the number is certainly far lower than estimates put forward by Hamas and its supporters. Even if it is as high as twenty-three thousand—the forty thousand–plus total claimed by Hamas minus the seventeen thousand–plus combatants Israel says it has killed—that would produce a ratio of civilians to combatants killed of less than two-to-one—that is, for every combatant killed, fewer than two civilians would have been killed.

If this ratio is close to being true, then Israel's record is far better than that of any other country in the history of modern urban warfare facing comparable enemies and tactics. Typical ratios of civilian to combatant deaths range from three-to-one to ten-to-one, as in the cases of Afghanistan, Iraq, Yemen, and Syria. And those ratios occur in situations where civilians are not used as human shields and in urban warfare.

This brings us to the law of war. The only requirement of proportionality under international law is that when combatants are targeted in areas where civilians are present, the value of the military target must be proportional to the number of anticipated civilian deaths. This highly subjective judgment cannot be the basis of a war-crime prosecution, unless the judgment is utterly unreasonable. The less than two-to-one ratio achieved by Israel is not only reasonable, but far better than that achieved by other armed forces facing comparable situations. Thus, were Israel to be prosecuted for violating the principle of proportionality, that would necessarily involve the application of a double standard against the Jewish state.

The charge of genocide made by South Africa is even less persuasive. Real genocides have taken place in the world today, especially in Africa. There is a genocide and deliberate starvation taking place in Sudan and Darfur today. South Africa has been silent about these neighboring genocides. And it is weakening the term itself by selectively politicizing it against Israel. Israel has provided health care to Gazans in need of Israeli hospitals. It provided high-paying jobs in Israel to thousands of Gazans. These are not the actions of a nation engaged in genocide.

Consider the preemptive attack Israel waged against Hezbollah rockets in late August 2024. The Airforce succeeded in destroying thousands of rocket launchers without killing any civilians. Or consider the explosive mechanisms planted in Hezbollah communication devices in September 2024. These devices were given by Hezbollah to its terrorists, who by definition are combatants. Only a tiny proportion of those killed or injured by the explosions were innocent civilians. The vast majority were active terrorists and their leaders. The same is true of Israel's targeted killing of Hezbollah and Hamas leaders.

Genocide is directed against an entire people, not just criminals and terrorists among them. To accuse Israel of genocide is to fail to distinguish between the legitimate military goal of ending a terrorist organization, such as Hamas, and the illegitimate goal of ending the existence of an entire ethnic or religious group.

The term genocide was coined to describe the Nazi effort to rid the world of all Jews. Accusing Israel of genocide is a form of Holocaust denial, since no one even suggests that Israel has extermination camps, gas chambers, or other mechanisms that exemplified the real genocide of the Holocaust. If Israel were to be found guilty of genocide, the very meaning of that horrible crime would be diluted beyond recognition. It would apply to the US bombing of Hiroshima, the British bombing of Dresden, and the killing of civilians during the Afghan, Iraqi, and Syrian military actions.

Every civilian death in wartime is a tragedy, and Hamas knew it was signing the death warrants of many civilians when it attacked Israel and then hid its war machinery among Gaza's civilian population. The death of a human shield is the legal and moral responsibility of those who deliberately placed civilians in harm's way. Consider the following example: A bank robber starts shooting at customers. When the police arrive, the robber grabs one of the customers and uses her as a human shield. A police officer, in an effort to save the lives of customers, tries to shoot the robber. But the hostage suddenly makes a move, and the police officer's bullet hits and kills her. Under the law of every nation, it is the hostage taker, not the policeman, who is guilty of killing the hostage, even though the bullet that killed her came from the police officer's gun.

It is Hamas, Hezbollah, and their Iranian patrons that should be on trial, not the victims of Hamas's barbarism.

Many military experts agree with John Spencer, Chair of Urban Warfare Studies at the Modern War Institute at West Point, that the "steps that Israel has taken to prevent casualties [in Gaza] is historic in comparison to all these other wars." The twenty-five-year military veteran has advised other Western democracies to follow Israel's example, because "Israel has taken more steps to avoid harming civilians than any other military in history."[22]

These steps include dropping leaflets and making phone calls to warn civilians of the targeting of areas from where terrorists are firing rockets or taking other military actions. They also include "roof knocking," which entails dropping noise-making warning devices on the roofs of buildings that the IDF plans to bomb.

---

22 John Spencer, "Israel Has Created a New Standard for Urban Warfare. Why Will No One Admit It?" *Newsweek*, March 26, 2024, www.newsweek.com/israel-has-created-new-standard-urban-warfare-why-will-no-one-admit-it-opinion-1883286.

These and other warnings create considerable military disadvantages and risks to the IDF. They give terrorists the opportunity to escape, to plant booby traps, to lie in ambush, and to take other actions that would otherwise be difficult or impossible. In other words, Israel is prepared to endanger the lives of their own soldiers to protect the lives of enemy civilians, even though some such "civilians" are almost certainly complicit in Hamas terrorism.

Why would Israel do that, especially since it is not required by the law of war? In part, for humanitarian reasons. But also for self-serving reasons: Israel's reputation, image, and support are weakened every time the IDF inadvertently kills a civilian. The IDF knows this. So does Hamas. That is why the IDF does everything reasonable to minimize civilian casualties—and why Hamas does everything in its power to maximize civilian casualties among the residents of Gaza, whose deaths they applaud. As a leader of Hamas once put it:

> For the Palestinian people, death has become an industry, at which women excel, and so do all the people living on this land. The elderly excel at this and so do the Mujahideen [i.e., a Muslim who fights on behalf of his faith] and the children. This is why they have formed human shields of the women, the children, the elderly, and the Mujahideen, in order to challenge the Zionist bombing machine. It is as if they were saying to

the Zionist enemy: "We desire death like you desire life."[23]

Israel does not deliberately target civilians. It does target terrorists who use civilians as human shields, and in pursuing such legitimate combatant targets, it does kill some civilians. This happens in every war, and especially in wars in which terrorists deliberately hide among civilians to achieve two purposes: making it more difficult for the IDF to target enemy terrorists, and getting the IDF to kill civilians in order to cast blame on Israel. The world must see through what I have called this "dead baby strategy"—using babies as human shields, so that their bodies can be paraded in front of the cameras.

As long as the world, encouraged by the media, continues to blame Israel for the death of civilians who are deliberately put in harm's way by Hamas and Hezbollah, this illegal and immoral use of human shields will continue, and more and more civilians will die.

---

23 "Hamas MP Fathi Hammad: We Used Women and Children As Human Shields," February 29, 2008, The Middle East Media Research Institute (MEMRI), www.memri.org/tv/hamas-mp-fathi-hammad-we-used-women-and-children-human-shields.

6. The Accusation: "Israel Is Engaging in Forced Starvation"

The Reality: There is no starvation in Gaza. To the contrary, Israel has done more to feed the civilians of Gaza than any nation while responding to the deadliest attack on Jews since the Holocaust.

The International Criminal Court of Justice (ICC) brought charges against Prime Minister Netanyahu and Yoav Gallent accusing them of forced starvation of civilians as a method of warfare.

In its indictment, the ICC relied heavily on a March 2024 report by the key Integrated Food Security Phase Classification (IPC) organization, which had warned that a famine would break out between March and July 2024. By June 2024, no reported deaths had occurred as the result of starvation. The study was later revised, stating that assumptions in the previous model were wrong and acknowledging that the supply of food to Gaza has increased rather than decreased between March and June 2024.

The truth is that Israel is not the reason why food and aid did not reach the Palestinian civilian population. Hamas is. In the first six months since October 7, Israel and its allies provided nearly 375,000 tons of humanitarian aid to Palestinian civilians, through land, air, and sea. Eighteen thousand trucks have carried aid into Gaza. Israel, and with the help of its allies, airdropped more than 1,200 packages to northern Gaza. Are these the actions of a country that employs starvation as a means of warfare? By contrast, Hamas has blocked entry of food, stolen it, and even attacked food trucks designated for Gaza's civilian population.

There is a real starvation going on in places such as Sudan. As *The New York Times* recently reported in an article titled "As Starvation Spreads in Sudan, Military Blocks Aid Trucks at Border,"[24] as many as 2.5 million Sudanese may die as a result of starvation by the end of 2024. The Sudanese military refuses to allow UN aid convoys to enter. Out of the fourteen Sudanese districts at immediate risk of famine, eight are in Darfur, the region whose conflict George Clooney and other members of the Hollywood elite have called the world's attention to. Yet now, as the country is facing one of the world's worst famines in decades, Clooney as well as other members of the liberal elite are suspiciously silent.

The silence of some leaders in the Black community is

---

24 Declan Walsh, "As Starvation Spreads in Sudan, Military Blocks Aid Trucks at Broder," *New York Times*, July 26, 2024.

also deafening. Immediately after October 7, before Israel engaged in any kind of military response, Black Lives Matter across the US universally sided with Hamas. As the war went on, Black Lives Matter leaders, as well as those of other prominent Black activist groups, accused Israel of war crimes, including genocide, while not expressing comparable concern for the situation in Sudan.

Why is the ICC singling out Israel, while not doing more to address the dire situation in Sudan? The ICC has failed its aspiration to be a neutral court of objective law and instead it chose to become a partisan court of "politics."

According to its own founding documents, the ICC is precluded by the treaty that created it from investigating any individual from a state that is willing and able to conduct a genuine investigation of that person. Israel is conducting ongoing investigations of alleged war crimes and will continue to do so.

One of the central tenets of the rule of law is that courts must comply with the limits on their jurisdiction imposed by the authorities that created them. The International Criminal Court is the creation of the Rome Statute, which severely limited its jurisdiction by the rule of complementarity. This rule expressly denies the ICC the authority to be the primary investigator or prosecutor of any individual who is subject to legitimate investigation and prosecution by his or her nation.

The ICC secures complementary jurisdiction only if

the nation with primary jurisdiction is unwilling or unable to conduct a fair and thorough investigation.

The signatories of the Rome Statute envisioned cases where the national judicial system had either totally or partially collapsed; is unable to "obtain an accused or key evidence and testimony"; or is "unable to carry out its proceedings"[25] because it lacked "sufficient qualified personnel to effect a genuine prosecution." The signatories of the Rome Statute did not envision a primary investigation of a Western democracy, such as Israel, whose Supreme Court has been called "the most activist judicial body of any advanced nation in the world."[26]

Unless the criteria for admissibility under Article 17 of the Rome Statute are satisfied, which they clearly are not here, the ICC simply has no authority to investigate or prosecute any alleged crime that can and will be investigated by Israeli authorities. To do so would be to violate its own charter and place itself above its own law.

According to the preamble of the Rome Statute, the International Criminal Court "shall be complementary to national criminal jurisdictions." Under the principle of complementarity, the ICC has jurisdiction only if a state

---

25 Rome Statute of the International Criminal Court, Article 17.

26 Shayndi Raice, "The Judge at the Heart of Israel's Constitutional Crisis," *Wall Street Journal*, June 30, 2023.

is either "unwilling or unable to genuinely carry out the investigation or prosecution."[27]

This was the original intent of the drafters of the Rome Statute. As legal scholars Michael Reisman and Mahnoush Arsanjani point out, "before and during the Rome negotiations . . . it was assumed that the court would become involved only in those states that were unwilling or refused to prosecute, staged a sham prosecution of their governmental cronies, or were simply unable to prosecute."[28]

Many signatories would not have agreed to the Rome Statute had the International Criminal Court been given jurisdiction to initiate investigations or prosecutions when the countries with primary jurisdiction were willing and able to investigate war crimes themselves.

Israel's judicial system is among the best in the world and its Supreme Court is among the most highly regarded of any Western democracy. Its judicial system has consistently stood up for the civil liberties of its people, including minority groups. It has put soldiers and settlers on trial and even prosecuted former (and current) political leaders, including three prime ministers and one president.

Under no reasonable definition of Article 17 can Israel's judicial system be considered "collapsing." Since

---

27 Rome Statute of the International Criminal Court, https://legal. un.org/icc/statute/99_corr/cstatute.htm.

28 Mahnoush H. Arsanjani and W. Michael Reisman, "The Law-In-Action of the International Criminal Court," *American Journal of International Law*, Vol. 99:385, 2005.

Israel is willing and able to investigate and, if necessary, prosecute any allegations of war crimes, the ICC is precluded from initiating an investigation against Israel.

Moreover, Israel is not a signatory to the Rome treaty, and neither Hamas nor the Palestinian Authority are states. But even if the ICC can overcome these hurdles (as it has claimed), it cannot overcome its own barrier to investigating alleged crimes committed by individuals who can be and are being held accountable by their own nations.

Israel is not Hamas, and the rules of the ICC are not the same for democracies that live under the rule of law and terrorist groups that live under the rule of lawlessness. Unfortunately, the ICC fails to recognize this distinction and has become an instrument of the international community that has always imposed—and continues to impose—a double standard on the only Jewish state in the world.[29]

---

29 In a recent *New York Times* op-ed, Bret Stephens surveyed the human rights abuses on Venezuela, Turkey, Sudan, and Iran and wrote: "Of all the world's injustices, perhaps the saddest is that so many of them are simply ignored. Protesters the world over loudly demand a cease-fire in Gaza; a dwindling number of people still take note of Russian atrocities against Ukraine. Otherwise, there's a vast blanket of silence, under which some of the world's worst abusers proceed largely unnoticed and unhindered." Bret Stephens, "Can We Be a Little Less Selective with Our Moral Outrage?" *New York Times*, Aug 27, 2024.

7. The Accusation: "Israel Engages in Illegal Occupation of Palestinian Territory"

The Reality: Israel's occupation of Palestinian territory is not unlawful.

It is clearly established, by international law and the law of war, that a military occupation that resulted from a legitimate war may continue as long as belligerency persists. When the allies occupied Germany and Japan following the defeat of the Nazi and imperialist regimes, belligerency quickly abated. Nonetheless, the occupations went on for seven years in the case of Japan and eleven years in the case of Germany. Had the defeated soldiers offered resistance, the occupation would have gone on much longer.

There can be no doubt that in the West Bank and Gaza, resistance and belligerency persist. Terrorist organizations, cells, and individuals fire rockets, plant bombs, shoot, stab, and ram Israeli soldiers and civilians both in Israel proper and in the territories. Israel has the right, indeed the obligation, to protect its civilians by maintaining a military occupation.

In an effort to promote peace, Israel made a mistake by ending its military occupation of the Gaza Strip—as distinguished from its civilian settlements—in 2005. The result has been thousands of rockets, terrorist attacks, and most recently the barbarisms of October 7.

It should not repeat that mistake by unilaterally ending its military presence on the West Bank, while terrorism persists. It repeatedly offered to do so in exchange for peace, but these offers were not accepted. Until belligerency ends on the West Bank, the military occupation must continue, because it is necessary to save lives.

The civilian settlements raise different and more complex issues, to which we now turn.

8. The Accusation: "Israel's Illegal Settlements in the West Bank Are a Barrier to Peace"

The Reality: Israel's settlements in the West Bank are no barrier to peace.

The issue of civilian settlements in occupied territories raises different and more controversial and nuanced issues. The resolution of these issues depends on several disputed factors.

The first is whether the West Bank is "occupied" as distinguished from "disputed," territory. Scholars disagree. Those who argue that it is not "occupied," as a matter of international law, point to the fact that this area never rightfully "belonged to" any recognized, legitimate political entity. It was captured by the British from the Turks during World War I and became part of the British mandate. The UN then proposed that it become the Arab part of a two-state solution. The Arabs rejected the UN proposal and attacked Israel. Following the war of independence, Jordan illegally occupied the West Bank until it was captured from them by Israel after Jordan unlawfully attacked Jerusalem in 1967. Since then, it has been subject to dispute.

In Resolution 242 of the UN Security Council, Israel was required to return "territories"—not all territories—it captured from Jordan. But Jordan did not want the West Bank back. It allocated it to Palestine, a non-existent abstract entity with no governing body that was "ruled" by terrorists. Now the Palestinian Authority claims it, but has been unwilling to negotiate a resolution that would have given it more than 90 percent of the disputed land in exchange for recognition and peace with Israel.

That is the current, disputed, and unresolved status of the West Bank. Under these circumstances, and with this complex history, it cannot be stated categorically that all the civilian settlements on the West Bank are clearly illegal. Consider, for example, the Etzion Block.

The Etzion Block, which is just South of Jerusalem, has been disputed since it was first established, before the creation of Israel on May 14, 1948. Beginning in 1947, Arab armies laid siege to the Jewish communities in the block, and on May 13, 1948, after its residents surrendered and came out with the heads up, the Arab fighters massacred 127 of them.

When Israel retook the block in 1967, descendants of the original residents asked Israel's labor government to resettle the area, and the government agreed. That was the first civilian settlement. Many others followed, and

there are now approximately five hundred thousand settlers (not including two hundred thousand Israelis living
in East Jerusalem) on 40 percent of the West Bank. In
2001 and 2007, Israel offered to limit civilian settlements
to less than 10 percent of the area of the West Bank in
exchange for peace.[30] The Palestinian leadership did not
accept the offer or even make a counteroffer, and more
settlements followed.

I have opposed the expansion of civilian settlements
as a matter of policy, but I regard their legality as a matter
of reasonable disagreement, as does the United States. As
former Secretary of State Mike Pompeo said: "The United
States is expressing no view on the legal status of any individual settlement,"[31] and it has not joined UN resolutions
declaring those settlements illegal. Much of the rest of the
international community regards all the civilian settlements as illegal. When I met with Mahmoud Abbas, he
agreed that any reasonable resolution of the dispute would
allow Israel to retain control over certain settlements—
those adjoining Jerusalem—but not of the vast majority
of them.

The bottom line is that many of the settlements, par-
ticularly those in the heart of the West Bank, would have
to be dismantled in the event of a peaceful resolution that

---

30 There were numerous proposals but none exceeded 10 percent.

31 John Hudson, "Trump Administration Says Israel's West Bank
    Settlements Do Not Violate International Law," *Washington Post*,
    Nov. 18, 2019.

led to a two-state solution. When Israel left the Gaza Strip in 2005, it dismantled all of the civilian settlements there and required its nine thousand Israeli residents to leave. The same could be done on the West Bank, though not without controversy, if the Palestinian leadership were to agree to a peace deal in the West Bank.

9. The Accusation: "Israel Is Preventing a Two-State Solution"

The Reality: Hamas, Hezbollah, and Iran, not Israel, are the barrier to peace and a two-state solution.

No two-state solution—indeed no solution that includes Israel's continued existence—is possible if Hamas remains in political and military control of the Gaza Strip, and Hezbollah maintains control over Lebanon. Hamas has stated its goal unambiguously: the political and military destruction of Israel, and the substitution of an Islamic state from the Jordan River to the Mediterranean Sea. The same is true of Hezbollah and Iran. They brook no compromise with what they regard as its religiously mandated delegation. Its leaders and followers are prepared to die, and have their families and associates die, in order to achieve that goal. They cannot accept any solution short of this final solution as a permanent end of hostilities. They can compromise over cease-fires, prisoner exchanges, and other temporary ameliorative solutions, but not over the only permissible permanent solution for them: the end of any Jewish political presence in what they claim is Muslim religiously ordained land that can never be a part of a Jewish state.

Although the Palestinian authority has thus far refused to agree to a compromise that would create a two-state solution, in principle it is open to that possibility. Indeed, Mahmoud Abbas has criticized past Palestinian leaders who rejected the UN Partition Plan of 1947, that would have led to a two-state solution. In his recent appearance before the UN General Assembly, Abbas called for the expulsion of Israel from the United Nations. Hamas praises all Palestinian rejectionism of any compromise that would allow Israel to continue to exist as the nation-state of the Jewish people. Accordingly, if there is to be any hope of a realistic peace process that includes the Gaza Strip, Hamas cannot remain in control. Indeed, Hamas is a barrier even to a peace process limited to the West Bank, because Hamas might well win an election on the West Bank.

Some argue that even if Hamas and Hezbollah are defeated militarily, it is impossible to defeat its ideology. History has proved that view wrong. When the German Nazis and Japanese imperialists were defeated militarily, their ideologies were rejected by the vast majority of German and Japanese survivors of their military defeat. It is certainly possible that the survivors of a Hamas military defeat would reject the ideology that brought so much suffering to the people of Gaza. That would be more likely if the international community helped rebuild Gaza, as it helped rebuild Germany and Japan after the war. That is the best hope for a compromise solution that would benefit all in that part of the world.

10. Claim: "Iran Is Not a Barrier to Peace"

The Reality: Iran is the main barrier to regional peace.

Iran is the key player in its current warfare in the Middle East. It controls Hamas, Hezbollah, the Houthis, and other terrorist groups that attack Israel on a regular basis. It too has attacked Israel directly. It controls "the ring of fire" that surrounds Israel and endangers its security. If Iran were to develop a nuclear arsenal, these groups would be able to operate from under an Iranian nuclear umbrella, which would make the prospects for peace even more distant than it seems today.

The best, but unlikely, solution to this problem would be regime change from the Mullahs to some form of democracy. The rule of the Shah, which ended in 1979, was far from democratic, but that regime did not export terrorism, as the current regime does. Nor did it seek the destruction of Israel, as the current regime does. Indeed, for all its faults—and there were many—it cooperated with the United States, Israel, and other nations in the region. Shortly after the 1979 religious revolution, Iran engaged in an eight-year war with Iraq that disrupted the region. This was followed by many more disruptive actions by Iran that persist today.

There is no realistic possibility for an overarching peace in the region so long as Iran remains the primary exporter of terrorism. Matters will only get worse if Iran were to develop a nuclear arsenal, which it would be capable of using not only as a defensive umbrella, but also as an offensive weapon against Israel. Hashemi Rafsanjani—the former "moderate" President of Iran—threatened Israel with nuclear destruction, boasting that an Iranian attack would kill as many as five million Jews. Rafsanjani estimated that even if Israel retaliated by dropping its own nuclear bombs, Iran would probably lose only fifteen million people, which he said would be a small "sacrifice"[32] from among the billion Muslims in the world. "He seemed pleased with his formulations."[33] Former president Mohammad Khatami has threatened to use Iran's missiles to destroy Jewish and Christian civilization: "Our missiles are now ready to strike at their civilization, and as soon as the instructions arrive from the leader Ali Khamenei, we will launch our missiles at their cities and installations."[34]

---

32 Quoted in Alan Dershowitz, *The Case for Peace*, Ch. 13 "Is The Iranian Nuclear Threat A Barrier to Peace?" (2005).

33 Ibid.

34 Ibid.

Khatami has in turn urged his military to "have two nuclear bombs ready to go . . . or you are not Muslims." The Iranian military has paraded its missiles through the streets of Tehran. These missiles, which can reach Israel, were draped with banners that read CRUSH AMERICA and WIPE ISRAEL OFF THE MAP.

Many in Israel, including centrists, have urged the IDF to take preemptive military steps to destroy Iran's nuclear weapons program before it becomes operational. Whether or not it takes such a risky step, Iran will remain the most significant barrier to regional peace unless there is regime change or an unlikely alteration in its policies.

Concluding Question: Why Does the Hard Left Champion Palestinianism over Other More Righteous Causes?

In a world in which massive violations of human rights have, tragically, become the norm, why has the hard left focused on one of the least compelling of those causes—namely, the Palestinians? Where is the concern for the Kurds, the Chechens, the Uyghurs, the Sudanese, the Tibetans? There are no campus demonstrations on their behalf, no expressions of concern by "the Squad" in Congress, no United Nations resolutions, no recurring op-eds in *The New York Times*, and no claims that the nations that oppress these groups have no right to exist.

On the merits and demerits of their claims, the Palestinians have the weakest case. They have been offered statehood and independence on numerous occasions: in 1937–1938, 1948, 1967, 2000–2001, and 2007. Israel ended its occupation of the Gaza Strip in 2005. Yet, even now, Palestinian leaders refuse to sit down and negotiate a reasonable two-state solution. As the late Israeli diplomat Abba Eban once aptly put it, the Palestinian leadership never misses an opportunity to miss an opportunity.

Nor are history and morality on their side. The Palestinian leadership allied itself with Nazism and Hitler in the 1940s, with Egyptian tyranny and anti-Semitism in the 1950s, and with international terrorism from the 1960s forward.

In 1947, the United Nations divided the land that the Romans called Palestine, and the Jews called Yisrael into two areas. It provided a sliver of land along the Mediterranean and a non-arable desert called the Negev to the Jews, who were a majority in that area, and a much larger arable area to the Arabs. The Jews declared statehood on their land. Instead of declaring statehood on their land, the Palestinians and surrounding Arab nations declared war. The Arabs lost and the Jews captured more land. As a result of the war, there occurred an exchange of populations: hundreds of thousands of Arabs left or were forced out of Israel, and hundreds of thousands of Jews left or were forced out of Arab countries and Arab Palestine.

Again, in 1967, the surrounding Arab nations threatened to destroy Israel, which preemptively attacked and occupied the West Bank and Gaza, which it immediately offered to return—with some territorial adjustments necessary for security—in exchange for peace and recognition. The UN Security Council issued Resolution 242, which called for a return of captured territories in exchange for peace. Israel accepted. The Arab nations and the Palestinians, however, issued their three infamous "no's"—no peace, no recognition, no negotiation.

The Kurds have never been offered independence or statehood, despite treaties that promised it. Nor have the Tibetans, the Uyghurs, or the Chechens. But the Palestinians have, on multiple occasions since 1938, when their leader told the Peel Commission that the Palestinians don't want a state—they just want there not to be a Jewish state.

The Palestinian people have suffered more from the ill-advised decisions of their leaders than from the actions of Israel.

Back to the present: Hamas and Hezbollah commit double war crimes every time they fire lethal rockets at Israeli civilians from areas populated by their civilians, who they use as human shields. Israel responds proportionally in self-defense, as President Biden has emphasized. The Israel Defense Forces go to extraordinary lengths to try to minimize civilian casualties among Palestinians, despite Hamas's policy of using civilian buildings—hospitals, schools, mosques, and high-rise buildings—to store, fire, and plan their unlawful rockets and incendiary devices. Yet the hard left blames Israel alone, and many on the center left create a moral equivalence between democratic Israel and terrorist Hamas.

Why? The answer is clear and can be summarized in one word: Jews.

Conclusion

Debate about the Middle East conflict is essential, especially on university campuses. But constructive debate requires objective truth, not biased lies. My hope is that this book will contribute to honest dialogue and compromise solutions that benefit all Israelis and Palestinians, and will promote peace.

The enemy of the Kurds, the Tibetans, the Uyghurs, and the Chechens are not—unfortunately for them—the Jews. Hence, there is little concern for their plight. If the perceived enemy of the Palestinians were not the Jews, there would be little concern for their plight as well. This was proved by the relative silence that greeted the massacre of Palestinians by Jordan during "Black September" in 1970, or the killings of Palestinian Authority leaders in Gaza during the Hamas takeover in 2007. There has been relative silence, too, about the more than four thousand Palestinians—mostly civilians—killed by Syria during that country's current civil war. It is only when Jews or their nation are perceived to be oppressing Palestinians that the left seems to care about them.

While the United States provides financial support for Israel, we also provide massive support for Jordan and Egypt. Even if the United States were to end support for Israel, the demonization of Israel by the hard left would not end.

The Left singles out the Palestinians not because of the merits of their case but, rather, because of the alleged demerits of Israel and the double standard universally applied to Jews. That is the sad reality.

Former CIA director John Brennan as much as admitted this double standard when he complained in a tweet about the alleged lack of empathy by Jews: "I always found it difficult to fathom how a nation of people deeply scarred by a history replete with prejudice, religious persecution, & unspeakable violence perpetrated against them would not be the empathetic champions of those whose rights & freedoms are still abridged."[35]

As Seth Frantzman, a writer for the *Jerusalem Post*, aptly put it: "In his telling of it, he implied that Jews must have special empathy for others while non-Jews have no special need to be empathetic. Brennan has not . . . held other countries to a higher standard based on the ethnic and religious origins of their citizens. . . . In short, because Jews endured genocide, they have to live according to a higher standard than those who perpetrated genocide."[36]

This "benevolent" double standard may sound kinder than the malevolent double standard imposed by members of "the Squad" and others, but it has the same effect: it demands that Israel do less to protect its citizens from rockets and terrorism than is demanded from other countries. To the contrary, the same standard must be demanded of Israel as is demanded of other countries defending their citizens. In particular, the same standard must be demanded of Palestinians and their leaders as is demanded of other groups seeking the moral support of good people.

As of now, the Palestinians have failed to meet that standard.

The legitimate rights of Palestinians to a peaceful state

35 Michael Brendan Dougherty, "Why Isn't John Brennan in Prison?" *National Review*, April 28, 2021.

36 Seth J. Frantzman, "Former CIA Head Targets Jewish Suffering in Israel's Actions—Analysis," *Jerusalem Post*, April 29, 2021.

over time should be supported, not so much because their history and actions merit it more than others, but because it would be good for peace in the region and for Israel. But it should not be prioritized over other more, or equally, compelling claims just because Jews are on the other side. Protesters who claim to be "pro-Palestinian" should look themselves in the mirror and ask, "why have you prioritized the morally weak Palestinian cause over far more just causes?" The honest answer should be clear to any objective observer: because the Jews and their nation-state are being subjected to an invidious double standard. That is morally, legally, and politically unacceptable for universities, students, politicians, citizens, and any who believe in equal treatment without regard to race, religion, ethnicity, or other statuses. The Jewish people and their nation-state are entitled to equal protection.

I was recently sent a T-shirt that should be worn by all the bigoted hypocrites who focus only on Israel's imperfections:

I am not that interested in the repression and human rights abuses in Syria, Togo, Iran, China, Yemen, Venezuela, Burkino Faso, Somalia, Eritrea, Bangladesh, Saudi Arabia, Cameroon, Turkmenistan, Libya, Sudan, Zimbabwe, Equitorial Guinea, North Korea and Russia—if there are no Jews involved!

Anti-Semite International